Jazz Etudes Over Classic Jazz Changes

by George Benson

ISBN 0-7935-8512-0

Houston
PUBLISHING, INC.

EXCLUSIVELY DISTRIBUTED BY

HAL•LEONARD®
CORPORATION
7777 W. BLUEMOUND RD. P.O. BOX 13819 MILWAUKEE, WI 53213

Acknowledgements

I would like to thank my son Michael Benson for his help and ideas on the computer.

I would also like to thank Steve Shepard for his help in making up the formula for the permutations.

6

7

10

11

12

14

16

18

20

22

23

24

26

28

29

30

32

33

36

37

39

40

41

42

43

44

45

48

49

52

54

55

57

58

59

60

61

62

63

64

65

66

68

69

About the Author

GEORGE BENSON has played at the Montreux Jazz Festival in Switzerland and Detroit, the Olde Time Jazz Festival in Breda Holland, the Toronto Jazz Festival, and the Ottowa Jazz Festival.

Other experience includes having played with many well known artists such as Tommy Flanagan, Barry Harris, Errol Garner, Sonny Stitt, Gene Ammons, Hank Jones, Thad Jones, Elvin Jones, Kenny Burrell, Yusef Latef, J.C. Heard, Frank Marocco. He has also backed Tony Bennett, Lena Horne, Ella Fitzgerald, Mel Torme, Dinah Washington, Sammy Davis, Milton Berle, and many more.

George was also featured on the albums "The Detroit Tradition Alive and Well" and "Detroit's George Benson Swings, and Swings, and Swings".

George Benson has taught jazz improvisation and theory at Henry Ford Community College and Schoolcraft Community College. He has given clinics at various colleges and high schools, and is currently on the applied music staff at Wayne State University.